Perfect Quotes for
COLLEGE SUCCESS

Perfect Quotes For COLLEGE SUCCESS

INSPIRATION, ADVICE, AND TIPS FOR ANYONE GOING TO COLLEGE

Tom Krieglstein

Illustrated By **Ona Rygelis**

Perfect Quotes for
COLLEGE SUCCESS

Tom Krieglstein

Illustrated By **Ona Rygelis**

A Swift Kick Book

Copyright © 2021 by Swift Kick

Perfect Quotes For
College Success

Printed in the United States of America

Written by Tom Krieglstein

Illustrated by Ona Rygelis

Editing by Jessi Ferguson

Quote curation by Justin Barker and Jay Chauhan

10 9 8 7 6 5 4 3 2

Swift Kick
www.SwiftKickHQ.com
sk@SwiftKickHQ.com
Phone: (877) 479-4385
Fax: (206) 337-0259

>> Contact for bulk order discounts <<

This book is dedicated to all students in college who are navigating through an exciting and challenging chapter in their life.

Table of Contents

Introd

Have you ever heard a quote that perfectly fit the situation or challenge you were facing? Sometimes all it takes is one simple quote to kick us mentally out of our rut and back into gear. This book is a handpicked collection of the perfect quotes for a variety of topics that someone entering, or already in, college might face. We scoured through thousands of quotes and selected only the very best for each topic in the hopes that when you read the perfect one, you'll have the ah-ha moment you need.

Unlike a traditional book that is read cover-to-cover, this book of quotes is meant to be picked apart. If your challenge today is around procrastination, then focus on that section. If tomorrow you are stressing out over switching majors, then flip there and find the perfect words to calm your nerves and get you focused again. You'll notice that the book's size, layout, and design are all intended to make this book be your ultimate college "coffee table book" that you can squeeze into a backpack or leave by your bed.

College can be one of the most exciting times of your life, and with this quote book as a supporting guide,

uction

College can be one of the most exciting times of your life, and with this quote book as a supporting guide, you'll find there is wise advice for every challenging topic you might encounter!

BEING A COMMUTER

It's easy to think that being a commuter puts you in the minority, but the reality is that as many as 83% of all college students nationwide commute to campus. You are the majority! Just because you are a commuter doesn't mean you are any less a member of the campus community, but it does mean you have to be just a little bit smarter in how you use your time while on campus.

Remember **to** **give** your**self** more than enough **time** to get **to** campus (weather, school busses, construction, etc...) **FOR** the **BEST** **PARKING.**

ALI BEARD

DON'T EAT LUNCH IN YOUR CAR! PENNY RUE

GET INVOLVED IN SOMETHING.

AS AN ACADEMIC ADVISOR THE MAJORITY OF THE COMMUTER STUDENTS SAY THEY FEEL DISCONNECTED.

STEPH MALONE

4

HAVE the mindset that the only difference between a commuter and a resident is where you sleep at night. Your

EXPERIENCE
IS WHAT you Make of it.

So TAKE advantage of every opportunity that is provided for all students.

AMY NOVAK

Try to get all of your classes on the same days.

No need to come to campus for just one class everyday.

ESTER WILSON

IT'S OKAY IF YOU DON'T HAVE TIME TO GET INVOLVED IN THE "TRADITIONAL" SENSE.

BALANCING CLASS AND WORK ISN'T EASY SO DON'T LET OTHERS MAKE YOU FEEL BAD ABOUT DOING WHAT YOU GOTTA DO TO

MAKE IT WORK.

ROHIT PRASAD

PARK CLOSEST TO YOUR LAST CLASS, NOT YOUR FIRST CLASS.

APRIL MARIE

Belon

02

Ging

A college campus is like a Petri dish of unlimited unique interests. Some students love sports; some could care less about sports. Some love Anime; others have never heard of it. Don't settle on the first group of people you meet. Keep exploring until you find a group of friends that are unique, wired, and cool, just like you. Only then will you be able to feel a sense of belonging because you will have found your crew.

Even if we ALL want YOU Here

YOU DON'T BELONG UNTIL

you DECIDE you do.

STEPHENIE MEYER

TO KNOW that you CAN NAVIGATE the WILDERNESS ON YOUR OWN - to KNOW that you can STAY TRUE to your beliefs, trust yourself, and SURVIVE IT - thats TRUE BELONGING.

BRENÉ BROWN

The **Heart** of the matter: you should never belong fully to something that is **Outside Yourself.** It is very important to find a BALANCE in your BELONGING.

JOHN
O'DONOHUE

IF THERE IS ANY **PRESSURE** TO SELL YOURSELF **CHEAP** YOU **TRULY** DON'T BELONG THERE.

EDMOND MBIAKA

WHEN **INSECURITY** STARTS TO **RUB OFF ON YOU**, YOU BEGIN TO LOOSE A SENSE OF **BELONGING**.

CHINONYE J. CHIDOLUE

BE THE
FLAMINGO
IN A FLOCK
OF
PIGEONS.
UNKNOWN

BEFORE BELONGING TO THE WORLD, YOU SHOULD BELONG TO YOURSELF, AS ONLY THOSE WHO ARE NOT HAPPY WITH THEIR OWN EXISTENCE SEARCH FOR IT OUTSIDE.

DR PREM JAGYASI

Cheating & Plagiarism

03

Cheating isn't just about doing something illegal; it's also a signal to the world about your character. It's never worth it, no matter how small, because the consequence at some schools is exceptionally severe. Nowadays, there are also sophisticated tools to catch plagiarism very easily. Instead of sacrificing your GPA, career, and character by cheating or plagiarizing, sacrifice your sleep or social life to do the work yourself.

BORROWED THOUGHTS LIKE BORROWED MONEY ONLY **SHOW** the **POVERTY** OF THE **BORROWER.** LADY MARGUERITE BLESSINGTON

Plagiarism results in SERIOUS CONSEQUENCES INCLUDING DICIPLINARY ACTION. Students CAN TAKE A Proactive approach. Check THEIR WORK for ISSUES before Submitting it TO THEIR INSTRUCTORS. TIMON L. KAPLE

17

Cheating in school is a FORM of Self Deception.

We go to SCHOOL to LEARN. We cheat OURSELVES when we coast on the EFFORST and Scholarship of someone else.

JAMES E. FAUST

I would prefer even to FAIL with HONOR than win by Cheating.

SOPHOCLES

PEOPLE WHO COPY YOU WILL

SATISFACTION lies in the EFFORT not in the ATTAINMENT. FULL EFFORT is FULL VICTORY.

MAHATMA GHANDI

ALWAYS BE ONE STEP BEHIND.
WAYNE GERARD TROTMAN

IF YOU **PLAGIARIZE** OTHERS' TECHNIQUES, YOU **STEAL THEIR EMOTIONS** AND TELL YOUR SPECTATORS A **LIE** WITH YOUR WORK.

WORKS AS SUCH EQUAL **ZERO.**

WU GUANZHONG

Dating & Love

04

Too many students spend far too much time majoring in dating while in school. And too many of those "true loves" only last a week and often require multiple days to recover from a broken heart. Instead of wasting your time trying to find the perfect person for you, spend the time making yourself into a better person. Then, the right person will come into your life and celebrate how amazing you are.

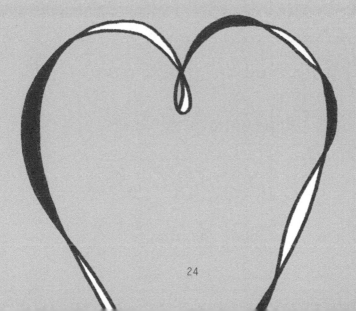

You Know
you're in love
when you can't
fall asleep
because
Reality is
finally better
than your
Dreams.
DR. SEUSS

WE ACCEPT
THE LOVE WE
THINK WE
DESERVE.

THE PERKS OF BEING A
WALLFLOWER

Don't Settle
for a Relationship
that won't let you
be Yourself.

OPRAH

SOMETIMES IT TAKES A HEARTBREAK TO SHAKE US AWAKE & HELP US SEE WE ARE WORTH SO MUCH MORE THAN WE ARE SETTLING FOR.

MANDY HALE

A healthier Relationship encompasses choosing Empathy over Ego.

STAN PEARSON

SEX IS ALWAYS ABOUT EMOTIONS. GOOD SEX is ABOUT fREE emotions; BAD SEX is ABOUT BLOCKED EMOTIONS.

DEEPAK CHOPRA

I DATED GUYS BECAUSE OF THE WAY THEY LOOKED. AND THEN I BEGAN TO LEARN THAT IT'S WHAT'S INSIDE THAT COUNTS. LOVE TO ME NOW IS UNDERSTANDING. IT'S GIVING.

CRYSTAL WATERS

DATING IN COLLEGE AND DATING IN HOLLYWOOD ARE ACTUALLY REALLY Similar IN THAT THE RELATIONSHIPS DON'T LAST LONG.

JULIA STILES

DIVER

05

SITY

When you come to college, expect to meet people from all over the world. Some people will share the same background as you, while others will have lived an entirely different life. Don't run or be scared of the diversity on campus; embrace it. Be like a sponge and try to learn from everyone, not just the people who are like you. Life is more interesting that way, anyway.

LEAVE YOUR COMFORT ZONE AND BECOME AQUAINTED WITH WORLD VIEWS THAT

DIVERSITY CREATES DIMENSIONS

DON'T
SYNC WITH YOURS.

LYNN O'SHAUGHNESSY

IN THE
WORLD.

ELIZABETH ANN
LAWLESS

It is TIME for Parents to TEACH young people early on that in diversity there is BEAUTY and there is STRENGTH.

MAYA ANGELOU

OUR ABILITY Unity IN diversity BEAUTY

When you EMBRACE **DIVERSITY** and **INCLUSION,** You SHOW how much you RESPECT an individuals UNIQUENESS.

FRANK KITCHEN

TO REACH WILL BE the & TEST OF OUR CIVILISATION.

Mahatma Gandhi

LEARNING ABOUT YOURSELF AND DIFFERENCES is like doing YOGA FOR THE FIRST TIME; IT MAY HURT INITIALLY BUT THE MORE YOU DO IT THE STRONGER & MORE FLEXIBLE YOU WILL BECOME.
STAN PEARSON

EVERYBODY IS A GENIUS.

BUT IF YOU JUDGE A FISH BY ITS ABILITY TO CLIMB A TREE, IT WILL SPEND ITS WHOLE LIFE BELIEVING THAT IT IS STUPID.

ALBERT EINSTEIN

DRUGS AND ALCOHOL

06

Just as you have the choice to pick the healthy sandwich at the cafeteria instead of the deep-fried cheese stick, you also have the choice not to use alcohol and drugs at social events. Yes, peer pressure will exist for you to participate; however, the choice will still be yours. As you will see in these quotes, many people go to college, have a fantastic time, and don't get lost in the harmful effects of alcohol and drugs.

I DON'T NEED ALCOHOL TO SEE THE WORLD IN IT'S DEPTHS, I CARRY THE SUN IN ME.

LAMINE PEARLHEART

I DO LIKE TO HAVE FUN.

Approximately ONE-FOURTH of college students report academic problems caused by excessive drinking such as missed classes or falling grades. SUSAN NEWMAN

I DO NOT NEED ALCOHOL TO HAVE FUN.
RIMA FAKIH

I am VERY SERIOUS ABOUT NO ALCOHOL, NO DRUGS.

MANY COLLEGE STUDENTS HAVE GONE TO COLLEGE AND GOTTEN HOOKED ON DRUGS, MARIJUANA, AND ALCOHOL.

LISTEN, STOP TRYING TO BE SOMEBODY ELSE. DON'T TRY TO BE SOMEONE ELSE. BE YOURSELF AND KNOW THAT THAT'S GOOD ENOUGH.

ROSIE WATSON

43

Life is TOO Beautiful."

JIM CARREY

Not drinking makes me a lot happier.

Naomi Campbell

WE DO NOT WANT TO BELIEVE THAT WE CANNOT CONTROL ALCOHOL AND THAT ALCOHOL IS, IN TRUTH, CONTROLLING AND DICTATING OUR LIVES. WHEN YOU FREE YOURSELF OF A DICTATOR, LIKE ALCOHOL, THE FREEDOM THAT YOU EXPERIENCE IS TOTALLY AMAZING AND EMPOWERING. YOU GET YOUR LIFE BACK.

LIZ HEMINGWAY

I HAVE SO STRONG A SENSE OF CREATION, OF TOMORROW, THAT I CANNOT GET DRUNK, KNOWING I WILL BE LESS ALIVE, LESS WELL, LESS CREATIVE THE NEXT DAY. ANAÏS NIN

Eating Well

You don't have to believe in the "Freshman 15" myth to know that at every meal, you have a choice as to how you are going to eat. Eating well isn't about eating healthy 100% of the time, but rather about being conscious about what, and how much, you are eating. You are on your own now, making your own choices about what you choose to put into your body.

To keep the health is otherwise be able to mind strong

A HEALTHY OUTSIDE STARTS FROM THE INSIDE.

ROBERT ULRICH

body in good
a duty,
we shall not
keep our
and clear.
BUDDHA

You dont
have to eat
Less, you just
have to
eat right.
UNKNOWN

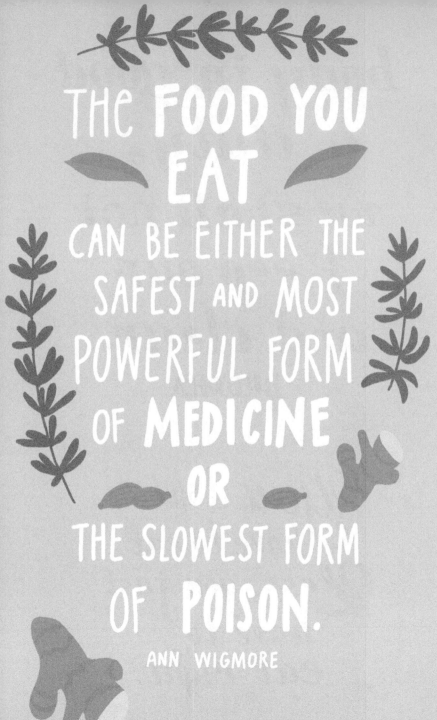

THE **FOOD YOU EAT** CAN BE EITHER THE SAFEST AND MOST POWERFUL FORM OF **MEDICINE** **OR** THE SLOWEST FORM OF **POISON.**

ANN WIGMORE

INVEST IN A
SLOW COOKER

THERE'S A TIMER ON IT, SO AS I'M PREPPING BREAKFAST IN THE MORNING, I CAN ALSO THROW ALL OF MY DINNER IN THE SLOW

COOKER AND SET THE TIMER. IT COOKS WHILE I'M GONE, THE FOOD STAYS WARM AND AS A RESULT, I CAN COME HOME AND JUST *SIT DOWN FOR DINNER.* KRISTI DAO

YOU CAN'T EXERCISE YOUR WAY OUT OF A BAD DIET.

MARK HYMAN

YOU ARE WHAT YOU EAT,

SO DON'T BE FAST, CHEAP, EASY, OR FAKE.

UNKNOWN

FINA

8

NCE$

Being broke in college is a given, so you better get used to dollar pizza and quarter tacos. While you might not have much money in your bank account, the financial habits you start building in college will show up for the rest of your life. Now is the time to start being smart with your money, whether you have a budget of $5 or $5,000.

Too many people spend money don't want... to impress people that

A BUDGET IS TELLING YOUR MONEY WHERE TO GO INSTEAD OF WONDERING WHERE IT WENT.

DAVE RAMSEY

Every time you borrow money, you're robbing

they earned... to buy things they they don't like. WILL ROGERS

JUST BECAUSE YOU CAN AFFORD IT DOESN'T MEAN YOU SHOULD BUY IT.

SUZE ORMAN

your future self.

NATHAN W. MORRIS

IF YOU THINK NOBODY CARES IF YOU'RE ALIVE, TRY MISSING A COUPLE OF CAR PAYMENTS.

EARL WILSON

I MIGHT LOSE THINGS, BUT I WILL NEVER LOSE THE EXPERIENCE. INVEST IN EXPERIENCES.

ROCKELL BARTOLI

BEWARE OF LITTLE EXPENSES, A small LEAK will SINK a GREAT SHIP.

BENJAMIN FRANKLIN

60

Finding a Job

At some point, you'll graduate from college and focus 100% on your career and getting a j-o-b. Waiting until graduation to think about finding a job is a big mistake that far too many students make. Don't wait. Start now and leverage your university's resources to get a jump start on finding a job and launching your career.

Most people who graduate from college think they have to make a PERFECT choice. Is it Goldman Sachs? Is it Google? Is it Apple? They think that their first job is going to determine their career, if not their life.

GUY KAWASAKI

• FIND OUT WHAT YOU *Like* DOING BEST AND GET SOMEONE TO PAY YOU FOR DOING IT.

KATHERINE WHITEHORN

THE ONLY WAY TO DO GREAT WORK IS TO LOVE WHAT YOU DO. IF YOU HAVEN'T FOUND IT YET, KEEP LOOKING. DON'T SETTLE. STEVE JOBS

A CAREER SHOULD BE YOUR CARE-AREA. FIND SOMETHING YOU CAN CARE ABOUT AND DO VERY WELL AND YOU'LL ALWAYS LOVE YOUR JOB. KENE IIOENYOSI

64

Getting fired is nature's way of telling you that you had the wrong job in the first place. HAL LANCASTER

Life's FIRST JOB is MUCH ADVENTUROUS AND

FOR MANY PEOPLE, THE HARDEST THING ABOUT JOB-SEEKING IS FIGURING OUT WHERE TO START. ALL THROUGH COLLEGE, I HEARD MY FRIENDS ASKING THEMSELVES, 'WHAT DO I WANT TO DO WITH MY LIFE?' AND GUESS WHAT? AFTER COLLEGE, AND AFTER THAT FIRST JOB, PEOPLE STILL ASK THE SAME QUESTION. KATHRYN MINSHEW

Like First Love... MAGICAL YET SOMETIMES FRUSTRATING BUT PRICELESS IN HINDSIGHT. ANONYMOUS

GETTiNG

10

INVOLVED

Your success in college, and life, is dependent on so much more than just going to class. Make it a point to get involved in the culture of the campus. Find a student club/organization that matches your interests and get involved. Research shows that your grades, graduation rate, and post-college income are all higher if you participate in at least one student organization.

A KEY PUSHED
Half-WAY iN
UNLOCKS NOTHING,

LIFE
always begins
with
one step
Outside of your
COMFORT ZONE.

SHANNON L. ALDER

BUT A *Key* PUSHED *All* the WAY UNLOCKS EVERYTHING.

GEO DERICE

IF YOU CAN **LEAD** WITHOUT RECOGNITION, **FOLLOW** WITHOUT **EGO** AND **LISTEN** WITHOUT JUDGEMENT, *you* **WILL SUCCEED** WITHOUT QUESTION.

STAN PEARSON

I make most of my FRIENDS THROUGH my EXTRACURRICULAR ACTIVITIES. KIERNAN SHIPKA

WHEN I WAS A TEENAGER, I BEGAN TO SETTLE INTO SCHOOL BECAUSE I'D DISCOVERED THE extracurricular ACTIVITIES THAT interested me: MUSIC AND THEATER.
MORGAN FREEMAN

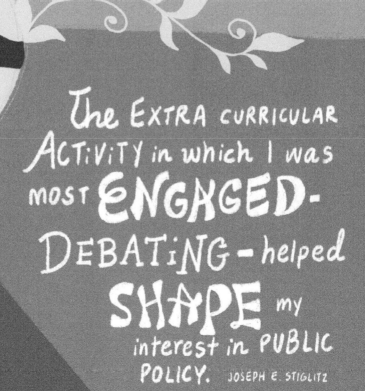

The difference between INVOLVEMENT and COMMITMENT is like HAM and EGGS. The chicken is involved; the pig is committed. MARTINA NAVRATILOVA

The EXTRA CURRICULAR ACTIVITY in which I was most ENGAGED - DEBATING - helped SHAPE my interest in PUBLIC POLICY. JOSEPH E. STIGLITZ

GOING TO CLASS

11

I know this sounds ridiculous to tell college students to go to class, but a daily reminder is needed for many students because the struggle is real. Don't pick early classes if you are a night owl, and don't pick night class if you are an early bird. Find a class schedule that works best for you, and you'll increase your chances of academic success.

EDUCATION IS THE MOST POWERFUL WEAPON

DON'T SET 5 ALARMS TO WAKE UP FOR YOUR 8 AM CLASS. JUST GET UP THE FIRST TIME. MARISSA NICOLE

WHICH YOU CAN USE TO CHANGE the WORLD. NELSON MANDELA

Education is the passport to the future, for tomorrow BELONGS to those who prepare for it today.

MALCOLM X

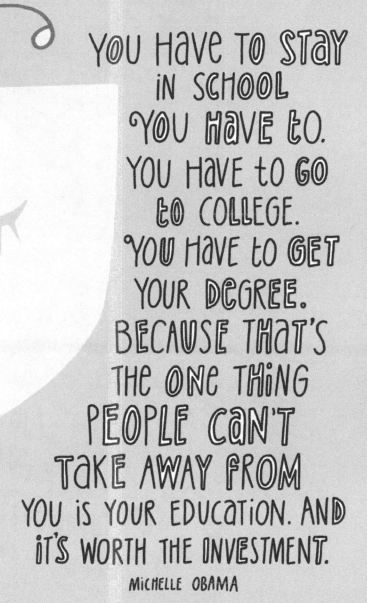

YOU HAVE TO STAY IN SCHOOL YOU HAVE TO. YOU HAVE TO GO TO COLLEGE. YOU HAVE TO GET YOUR DEGREE. BECAUSE THAT'S THE ONE THING PEOPLE CAN'T TAKE AWAY FROM YOU IS YOUR EDUCATION. AND IT'S WORTH THE INVESTMENT.

MICHELLE OBAMA

WHAT'S AMAZING is HOW DOING WELL in SCHOOL SO MUCH MORE INTERESTING,

WHEN YOU'RE A COLLEGE STUDENT ALL THESE RAPPERS TALKING WHEN I HEARD SOMEONE SCHOOL AND STAYING IN SCHOOL

YOUNG PEOPLE UNDERSTOOD MAKES THE REST OF THEiR LiFE THEY WOULD BE MORE MOTiVATED.

BiLL GATES

INTERESTED IN MUSIC, YOU HAVE ABOUT DROPPING OUT. FOR ME, LIKE J COLE RAPPING ABOUT IT INSPIRED ME TO KEEP GOING.

SAWEETE

GRADES

12

Grades are a necessary evil of an educational system dependent on ranking and quantifying how much a student learns. While it is true that post-college, almost no one will ask you about your grades, to ignore your grades while in college would be a failing behavior.

Everyone is told to GO TO HIGH SCHOOL and GET GOOD GRADES and GO TO COLLEGE and then GET A JOB and then GET A BETTER JOB. There's no one really telling a story about how they TOTALLY BLEW IT, and they FIGURED IT OUT.

SOPHIA AMORUSO

I was a **D** Student in high school and on the **DEAN'S** list in COLLEGE.

PATTI STANGER

We get GOOD GRADES OR POOR GRADES depending on our ATTITUDES.

STERLING W SILL

I DIDN'T
HAVE GOOD GRADES
UNTIL I STARTED
DANCING,

BECAUSE I DIDN'T
TRY - I DIDN'T SEE
the POINT.

ONCE I REALIZED
WHY I WANTED TO
GO TO COLLEGE,
I STARTED TO STUDY
AND DO WELL.

I KNEW I HAD TO
HAVE A CERTAIN GPA
TO GET IN.

KYLE ABRAHAM

FOR ME, ACTING WAS A REWARD. I HAD TO GET GOOD GRADES IN ORDER TO ACT, IN ORDER TO BE ON TV. I HAD TO DO WELL IN SCHOOL SO I COULD WORK. TO ME, IT WAS LIKE AN AFTER-SCHOOL ACTIVITY, SOMETHING TO LOOK FORWARD TO.

KYLA PRATT

I went to Columbia University because I knew I wanted to go to a school that was academically rigorous. I prided myself on getting good grades, but I also hated it.

EZRA KOENIG

87

GRADES do MATTER.

THERE MAY be FLAWS in many GRADING SYSTEMS, sometimes in the education SYSTEM itself, but the LETTERS AND NUMBERS do STILL HOLD VALUE.

IT May be a TOUGH TRUTH to swallow, but you're only HURTING YOURSELF if you PRETEND GRADES DON'T MATTER.

THERESE CASTRO

ATION

13

You made it! Some might say graduation is the end, but others might think of this as the beginning. Graduation marks a singular point in your life when all the hard work of schooling starts to pay off as you begin your career. Now you get to show the world what you learned and how you plan to put it to use while making your mark.

you cannot dream
you do not know
Learn to
Education exposes
world has TO OFFER, To the
TO YOU. SONIA SOTOMAYOR

WE DON'T STOP GOING TO
School when WE
GRADUATE. *CAROL BURNETT*

91

of becoming something about. You have to **Dream Big:** you to what the POSSIBILITIES OPEN

You have opportunities and skills and education that so many folks who came before you never could have dreamed of. So just imagine the kind of IMPACT that you're going to make. Imagine how you can INSPIRE those around you to reach HIGHER and complete their education.

MICHELLE OBAMA

So, I SAY TO YOU, FORGET ABOUT THE FAST LANE. IF YOU REALLY WANT TO FLY, JUST HARNESS YOUR POWER TO YOUR PASSION. HONOR YOUR CALLING. EVERYBODY HAS ONE. TRUST YOUR HEART AND SUCCESS WILL COME TO YOU. OPRAH WINFREY

Graduation is not the end; it is the Beginning.
ORIN HATCH

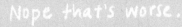

YOU ARE GRADUATING FROM college.

That means this is the first day of the last day of your life.

NO, that's wrong.

This is the last day of the first day of school.

Nope that's worse.

This is a day.

ANDY SAMBERG

YOUR Life is your STORY and the ADVENTURE AHEAD of you is the JOURNEY to FULFILL YOUR OWN PURPOSE AND POTENTIAL.

KERRY WASHINGTON

GREEK

Every student is consciously or unconsciously seeking friend groups happen randomly during orientation or of their way to pledge into a social group and become organization that builds you up to a better version of later on.

1

LIFE

to find a cohort of like-minded peers. Sometimes those

in the residence halls. Other times students will go out

part of the Greek Life on campus. The key is to find an

yourself, not bring you down to do things you'll regret

4

If as Sorority
and fraternity members,
we are unwilling to show
up for each other in the face
of ADVERSITY or be vulnerable
with one another in the face
of DISCOMFORT then we are
not doing Brotherhood
and Sisterhood
right.

TARA MICHELLE
FULLER

Being a part of
a fraternity has
given me the
foundation
for everything I do in my
career from the
loyalty to the
determination;
it laid the foundation
for everything I've been
able to
enjoy.

TERRANCE J

THE FINANCIAL COMMITMENT A SISTER MUST MAKE TO HER SORORITY CAN BE **ENORMOUS.**

ALEXANDRA ROBBINS

WHEN I WAS IN COLLEGE, I WASN'T IN A FRATERNITY OR ANYTHING. I ALWAYS WANTED TO JUMP AROUND TO DIFFERENT TYPES OF CLIQUES.

NICK GEHLFUSS

I'm the guy
who needs to be
FRONT & CENTER.
I joined a
FRATERNITY to
do that.
BERT KREISCHER

My Oldest friends today are my SORORITY SISTERS. The most important lesson I learned from being in a SORORITY is how to be a good friend. CLAUDIA WELCH

Joining a black sorority gave me sisters to lean on during college ~ a second family.

It also made me more involved in college activities.

JANIECIA MARSHALL

Joining my SORORITY was One of the MOST EXCITING DAYS, and this EYE OPENING experience has truly helped me find myself.

BRIANNA MARIE REYNOLDS

Home-sickness

15

If this is your first time living away from your family, it's very natural to feel a little homesick. It happens on every campus with many students, so don't feel alone. The good news is that with a bit of time, effort, and new positive experiences, you'll find your footing in college, and soon, you won't want to leave.

NO SHAME IN FEELING HOMESICK. IT MEANS YOU CAME FROM A

HAPPY HOME.

MRS. HUGHES

No matter where I go, I'll never forget home. I can feel its heartbeat a thousand miles away. Home is the place where I grew my wings.

BRENDA SUTTON ROSE

Avoid isolating yourself.

Walk around and get familiar with the campus and the surrounding areas, and find places you like to spend time.

ERIKA MARTINEZ

WHEN WE'RE FEELING BAD, OUR INCLINATION is TO RETREAT, INSTEAD, STUDENTS SHOULD OPEN THEMSELVES UP TO NEW EXPERIENCES. ITS important TO CREATE NEW RITUALS, FIND THE PLACE WHERE EVERYONE KNOWS YOUR NAME.

TAMAR CHANSKY

Maybe you had to leave in order to really *Miss a place;* *Maybe* you had to travel to figure out how Beloved your starting POINT **was.** JODI PICOULT

WHEN YOU GET HOMESICK, IT'S NOT SOMETHING MISSING, IT'S SOMETHING **Present, a Visit.** PEOPLE AND PLACES FROM FAR AWAY ARRIVE AND KEEP YOU **company** FOR A WHILE. ERRI DE LUCA

My father says
you remember the
smell of your
country no matter
where you are but
only recognize it when
you are
far away.

AGLAJA
VETERANYI

HOMEWORK

16

Homework isn't just about doing the work; it's about training your brain to stay focused, learning how to filter through massive amounts of information, and knowing the value of preparing before a big test. Treat homework like sleeping, eating, and breathing, because in college, you'll be doing it just as much.

One of life's most painful moments comes when we must admit that we didn't do our homework, that we are not prepared.

MERLIN OLSEN

IF YOU WANT TO BE LUCKY, DO YOUR HOMEWORK.

JIM ROGERS

A genius is a talented person who does his homework.

THOMAS A. EDISON

COLLEGE is
ABOUT THREE THINGS:
Homework,
Fun, AND
Sleep...
BUT YOU
CAN ONLY
CHOOSE
Two.
ANDY STERN

I like a teacher who gives you something to take home to think about besides homework.

LILY TOMLIN

LACK of HOMEWORK SHOWS UP IN THE MARKETPLACE AS WELL AS IN THE CLASSROOM.

JIM ROHN

The Same
did their homework
still doing that

out in the

REAL
WORLD.

JULES SHEAR

people who never
in high school are
to this very day

I WAS A
VERY GOOD STUDENT.
PROCRASTINATING GIVES
ME ANXIETY AND GETTING
a B REALLY TICKED ME OFF.
SURE I DIDN'T ALWAYS
WANT TO DO MY HOMEWORK
BUT I ACTUALLY REALLY LIKED
SCHOOL. AS NERDY AS IT SOUNDS,
I LOVE LEARNING.
JOSIE LOREN

17

If you thought your brother at home was gross, wait until you step inside a shared bathroom in your residence hall. From that moment on, you'll understand why shower shoes are so important and learn the value of keeping yourself and your living space clean.

Hygiene

GOOD HYGIENE ENHANCED (MY) SOUND WELL-BEING.

LAILAH GIFTY AKITA

THE GREATEST WEALTH IS HEALTH.

VIRGIL

If you don't SMELL GOOD then you don't LOOK GOOD.

KATY ELIZABETH

YOU KNOW WHAT i DO ALMOST EVERY DAY? i WASH. PERSONAL HYGIENE is PART OF THE PACKAGE WITH ME.
JiM CARREY

There has to be some Kind of personal hygiene bar that a person needs to clear in order for a relationship to be successful.
MALLORY ORTBERG

NOTHING INSPIRES

Nine-tenths of our sickness can be prevented by right thinking plus right hygiene–nine tenths of it. HENRY MILLER

KEEP YOUR OWN HOUSE AND IT'S SURROUNDINGS PURE AND CLEAN.

THIS HYGIENE WILL KEEP YOU HEALTHY AND BENEFIT YOUR WORLDLY LIFE.

SAI BABA

CLEANLINESS MORE THAN AN UNEXPECTED GUEST.

RADHIKA MUNDRA

INTERNSHIP

18

Internships are like test driving a car to see what make and model you like best. Be willing to try out several internships in different companies and even different careers. With each new internship, you'll learn a little more about what you like and don't like in a career path. Just remember to show up with your best self because interns tend to be a breeding ground for future hires.

THE IDEAL INTERN IS COMMITED, CREATIVE, ORGANIZED, AMBITIOUS, INDEPENDENT, AND ABLE TO CRACK A SMILE, WHETHER MEETING A CELEBRITY OR FOLDING SOCKS.

EMILY WEISS

Whenever you are ASKED if you can do a job, tell 'em, 'Certainly I Can!' THEN GET BUSY AND FIND OUT HOW TO DO IT.

THEODORE ROOSEVELT

DO INTERNSHIPS AND WORK YOUR BUTT OFF to LEARN AS MUCH AS YOU CAN AND PROVE YOURSELF.

MEREDITH VIEIRA

YOU DON'T HAVE to BE GREAT to START, BUT YOU DO HAVE to START TO BE GREAT.
ZIG ZIGLAR

Begin Somewhere. YOU CANNOT BUILD A REPUTATION ON WHAT YOU INTEND to DO.
LIZ SMITH

Create a LIST

OF YOUR INTENTIONS FOR
YOUR WORK.
THEN RESEARCH
AVAILABLE INTERNSHIPS
AND OR COMPANIES THAT
YOU ARE ATTRACTED TO
BASED ON THAT

Personal
NORTH STAR.

ONCE THAT IS CLEAR, YOU
BEGIN OUTREACH TO PEOPLE
CONNECTED TO INDUSTRIES
YOU'RE PASSIONATE AND/OR
Curious ABOUT.

CAROLINE GHOSN

SUCCESS DOESN'T COME TO YOU.

STUDY WHAT
you LOVE
and iNTERN in WHAT YOU
WANT   TO DO,
AND I tHiNK its OK to
PiVOT AS MANY times AS
YOU NEED TO.
EVA CHEN

YOU GO TO IT.

MARVA COLLINS

LIVING ON

19

CAMPUS

Living on campus can feel like a starter apartment for adulthood. The advantage is that you are now closer to the action and can quickly get to class and social events. But the trade-off is that most of the time you aren't living alone, you don't get to pick your roommate, and many common areas, like the bathroom, are shared.

Toto, I've a Feeling we're not in Kansas anymore.

DOROTHY

Wear Shower Shoes.

ABI WALSH

IN the MESSY world of a College dorm, I made a point to keep my ROOM neat and tidy.

These improvements were minor, BUT they gave me a SENSE of CONTROL OVER my life.

JAMES CLEAR

We decided we wanted our ROOM to smell like FRESH BAKED COOKIES. So we ordered a cookie-dough-scented candle off eBay,

and then we accidentally burn our room down with that candle.

DAVE FRANCO

IN YOUR DORM
YOU MEET MANY
NICE PEOPLE.

SOME ARE SMARTER
THAN YOU. SOME
ARE DUMBER THAN
YOU. YOU WILL
CONTINUE,
UNFORTUNATELY, TO
VIEW THE WORLD IN
EXACTLY THESE
TERMS FOR THE REST
OF YOUR LIFE.

LORRIE MOORE

HOME IS WHERE

or at least where

RAMEN.

UNKNOWN

DORM-ROOM
LIFE WAS A TOUGH
TRANSITION. YOU'RE
YOUNG AND YOU
REALIZE HOW

the HEART is...
you KEEP your

MUCH YOU MISS the
COMFORT OF HOME.
JORDAN BURROUGHS

LONELINESS

20

Even on a campus with 34,000 other people, a student can still feel lonely. The three best cures for loneliness are to find a group of friends, talk to a professional on campus about your feelings, or learn how to be your own best friend. All options are great but require a little effort on your part.

IF YOU'RE LONELY WHEN YOU'RE ALONE, YOU'RE IN

IF YOU ARE AFRAID OF BEING LONELY, DON'T TRY TO BE RIGHT.

JULES RENARD

At the innermost core of all lonliness is a DEEP AND powerful yearning for union with one's lost SELF.

BRENDAN BEHAN

141

I'VE NEVER THOUGHT ABOUT SONGWRITING AS a WEAPON. I'VE ONLY THOUGHT ABOUT IT AS A WAY TO HELP ME GET THROUGH LOVE AND LOSS AND SADNESS AND LONLINESS AND GROWING UP.

TAYLOR SWIFT

BAD COMPANY.

JEAN-PAUL SARTRE

Pray that your lonliness may spur you into finding something to Live for

The only time we WASTE is the time we spend thinking we are

Great enough to die for.
DAG HAMMARSKJOLD

ALL I EVER WANTED WAS TO REACH OUT AND TOUCH ANOTHER HUMAN BEING NOT JUST WITH MY HANDS BUT WITH MY HEART.

TAHEREH MAFI

alone.
MENITI BIANGLALA

MAKING

21

FRIENDS

College is as much a professional network of relationships as it is an academic institution. From the moment you start college through graduation and beyond, you'll have plenty of opportunities to make new friends and connections. Be willing to step outside your comfort zone to meet new people. Just make sure the friends you make will build you up instead of bring you down.

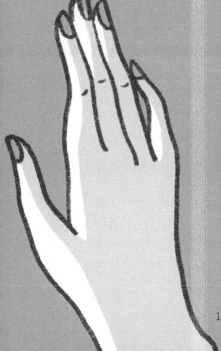

YOU CAN'T STAY in your CORNER of the FOREST WAITING

your VIBE

Be genuinely INTERESTED in everyone you meet and everyone you meet will be genuinely interested in you. RASHEED OGUNLARU

FOR OTHERS TO COME TO YOU.
YOU HAVE TO GO
TO THEM
SOMETIMES.
A. MILNE

ATTRACTS
YOUR TRIBE.
UNKNOWN

FRIENDSHIP is born at that moment when one PERSON says to ANOTHER, 'WHAT! YOU TOO? I thought I WAS THE ONLY ONE.

C.S. LEWIS

WE GET TO SUCCESS BY OUR RELATIONSHIPS AND THE WAY WE CARE FOR PEOPLE. VICKI ABADESCO

A friend may be waiting behind a STRANGERS face. MAYA ANGELOU

Show me your FRIENDS and i'll show you your FUTURE.

LEE BROWN

A REAL FRIEND is ONE WHO WALKS IN WHEN the REST of the WORLD WALKS OUT.

WALTER WINCHELL

Mental

22

Health

The most important thing to know about mental health is that you aren't alone. Just because we can't see mental illnesses like we can see a broken arm doesn't make them any less real or severe. Be willing to reach out and seek support. Most campuses have ample resources to support the mental health of their students.

It's
okay to not
be okay.

Sometimes it's hard to follow your heart. But tears don't mean you're losing, everybody's bruising,

There's nothing wrong with who you are! JESSIE J

STRESS
DOES NOT GO WITH
MY OUTFiT. UNKNOWN

The danger with regard
to mental health is a
student will try to self-
medicate ANXIETY,
DEPRESSION, OR OTHER
PROBLEMS WITH ALCOHOL AND
DRUGS. This just doesn't
work.
DR. SHERRY BENTON

Knock me down nine times, but I get up 10.

CARDI B

I found that, with depression, one of the most important things you could realize is that you are not alone.

DWAYNE JOHNSON

Perfection
is a disease
of a
Nation.

BEYONCÉ

Its OKAY to PUT
YOURSELF FIRST.
TRUST YOUR HEART
TO GUIDE YOU BACK
TO WHERE YOU
BELONG.

NHUNG HOANG

MOTiV

ATION

23

Every student could use an occasional boost. Sometimes the boost is to help them pull an all-nighter study session, to run a marathon, or just to get out of bed for a 7 a.m. class. While college can be a fantastic time, it can also be challenging and stressful. Don't let a little setback in attitude stop you from bouncing back better than ever.

If you can dream it, you can do it.

WALT DISNEY

You don't need a new day to start over. You only need a new *mindset*.

HAZEL MIRO OZBEK

We DO NOT NEED Magic to CHANGE the World. We carry all the POWER we need inside of ourselves already: We have the POWER to Imagine Better.

J.K. ROWLING

TRUST YOURSELF, YOU KNOW MORE THAN YOU THINK YOU DO.

BENJAMIN SPOCK

The DIFFERENCE between TRY and TRIUMPH is a little UMPH.

MARVIN PHILLIPS

WE SHOULD NOT GIVE UP AND WE SHOULD NOT ALLOW THE PROBLEM TO DEFEAT US. A.P.J. ABDUL KALAM

Wake UP with DETERMINATION

It always
seems impossible
until its
done.
NELSON MANDELA

and go to bed with
SATISFACTION.

UNKNOWN

24

Most students might not think about college as a networking gold mine, but it is. The people you will meet in college could be valuable connections for resources later in life. Your classmates might help you find a job, close a sales deal, or even fall in love. Treat each interaction with the long term in mind, and you'll start to realize how valuable networking at college can be.

ING

EVERYTHING YOU WANT IN LIFE IS A RELATIONSHIP AWAY.

IDOWU KOYENIKAN

YOUR NETWORK IS

YOUR NET WORTH.

PORTER GALE

Mingle OFTEN WiTH good PeoPLe to keep YOUR Soul NOURiSHED.

ANTHONY DOUGLAS WILLIAMS

NETWORKING is A LOT LIKE NUTRITION and FITNESS: WE KNOW WHAT TO DO, the HARD PART is MAKING it A TOP PRIORITY.
HERMINIA IBARRA

"It's the people we hardly know, and not our closest friends, who will improve our lives most DRAMATICALLY."

- MEG JAY

ITS IMPORTANT

TO BUILD A STRONG NETWORK BOTH IN YOUR PROFESSIONAL and PERSONAL LIFE.

OSCAR AULIQ-ICE

My GOLDEN RULE of Networking is simple: DON'T KEEP SCORE.

HARVEY MACKAY

OVERW

25

HELMED
/STRESSED

It's 2 a.m., and you just started studying for a test that makes up half your grade. Oh, and your best friend is mad at you. Don't panic, we've all been there. College and stress go hand in hand. The key isn't to live in a bubble and avoid stress because it's bound to happen. Instead, figure out how to embrace the pressure, learn from it, and move past it.

IF IT DOESN'T CHALLENGE YOU, IT WON'T

THERE IS A
FINE LINE
—— BETWEEN ——
CHALLENGING YOURSELF
AND **OVERWHELMING**
YOURSELF.
BRITTANY BURGUNDER

CHANGE YOU.

FRED DEVITO

YOUR PAST HAUNTS YOU
YOUR PRESENT OVERWHELMS YOU
YOUR FUTURE SCARES YOU
YET YOU SURVIVE.

LIDIA LONGORIO

SOMETIMES WHEN YOU'RE OVERWHELMED BY A SITUATION, WHEN YOU'RE IN THE **DARKEST** OF **DARKNESS** THAT'S WHEN YOUR **PRIORITIES** ARE **REORDERED.**

PHOEBE SNOW

It is nice finding that Place where you can just GO and Relax.

MOISES ARIAS

COLLEGE STRESS is A GIVEN AND CAN BE MANAGED BY EXERCISING Self CARe, eating healthy, getting enough sleep, AND ENGAGING IN SOME FORM OF STRESS - RELIEVING ACTiViTY.

SUSAN NEWMAN

Parents & Family

26

For many, college is the first time entirely away from their childhood roots. With this change comes a lot of mixed feelings for students. Your family is probably also going through their own set of emotions during this transition as well. As you explore life in college, try to remember where you came from and use that as a foundation for your future success.

FAMiLY means NO ONe gets left behind ~or~ forGOTTen.

DAVID OGDEN STIERS

MOMMA IS A SAINT, YES, SHE RAISED ME REAL GOOD.

DRAKE

CALL iT A CLAN, CALL iT A NETWORK, CALL iT A TRIBE, CALL iT A FAMILY: WHATEVER YOU CALL iT, WHOEVER YOU ARE, You need ONE.

JANE HOWARD

Other Things

If you LOVE SOMETHING,
(LIKE A SON GOING TO COLLEGE)
SET IT FREE.
JUST DON'T EXPECT
IT to come
back.

D.M. IRATOO

May CHANGE US, But we start and end WITH THE FAMILY.

ANTHONY BRANDT

FAMILY CAN MEAN PEOPLE YOU BROUGHT INTO YOUR LIFE TOO, NOT JUST PEOPLE YOU WERE BORN WITH.

DR. JESSICA CLEMONS

PARENTS are the bones on which CHILDREN CUT THEIR TEETH.

PETER USTINOV

PARENTS
aren't the people
you come from.

THEY'RE THE
PEOPLE
YOU WANT TO BE,

when
you grow up.

JODI PICOULT

27

No matter the day of the week, chances are there will be an opportunity to stop studying and start partying. The choice is yours to make, and it's part of growing up and becoming more responsible. Let's not go so far as to say don't party; instead, just remember that partying isn't the main reason you're here.

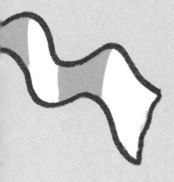

IF YOU'RE NOT INVITED TO THE PARTY

THROW YOUR OWN.

DIAHANN CARROLL

NEVER be the FIRST to arrive at a PARTY

Know your Limit. OFF CAMPUS Parties may PROViDE plenty of ALCoHOL, But you'll Let Your GUARD DOWN if you're drunk.

or the LAST to go HOME and NEVER, NEVER be both.

DAVID BROWN

SCHOOL
SHOULD BE THE
BEST PARTY IN
TOWN.
PETER KLINE

Life is the

Partying
is
such sweet
Sorrow.

ROBERT BYRNE

THE MORE YOU PRAISE AND Celebrate YOUR LIFE, the MORE there is in LIFE to CELEBRATE.

OPRAH WINFREY

Best Party I've been invited to.

- ARLENE FRANCIS

IF YOU'RE SPENDING YOUR ENTIRE early 20's CHASING the NEXT PARTY, what ARE YOU RUNNING AWAY FROM?

DEMI LOVATO

28

Patience

Take your time, young grasshopper. Don't try and do everything right now. Be willing to slow down and enjoy the moment. Four years of college might seem like a long time, but it goes by in the blink of an eye. Without the patience to appreciate each moment, the moments will be gone before you can say, "I graduated!"

With *love* and PATIENCE, nothing is impossible.

DAISAKU IKEDA

All GREAT ACHIEVEMENTS require time.

MAYA ANGELOU

The STRONGEST of all warriors are the TWO- TIME and PATIENCE.

LEO TOLSTOY

I AM A SLOW WALKER, BUT I NEVER WALK BACK.

ABRAHAM LINCOLN

192

TODAY'S PATIENCE CAN TRANSFORM YESTERDAY'S DISCOURAGEMENTS INTO TOMORROW'S DISCOVERIES.

WILLIAM ARTHUR WARD

PATIENCE YOU MUST HAVE, MY YOUNG PADAWAN.

YODA

Every great
dream begins
with a dreamer.
Always
remember,
You have
within YOU
the Strength, the Patience
and the Passion
to REACH for the STARS
and CHANGE the WORLD.

HARRIET TUBMAN

PICKING a MAJOR

29

Some students have known what they wanted to do from the time they told their kindergarten teacher their dream career. Other students will switch majors multiple times through college. There is no one right way to success. If you find yourself on a path that doesn't feel right, be willing to stop and reassess to see if maybe there is another path that's calling you more.

STUDY WHAT YOU LOVE. THE REST WILL FALL INTO PLACE.

UNKNOWN

S TUD**Y** the field that you want to get INT**O** and KNOW EVERYTHING ABOUT.

KIMORA LEE SIMMONS

The worst days of those who ENJOY what they do ARE BETTER than the BEST DAYS of those who dont.

GEORGE ELIOT

WHEN STUDENTS major in Subject areas that INTEREST them and they feel PASSIONATE about, they are more likely to ENGAGE FULLY with the material they are learning about. HELENA SANTOS

If you haven't found it yet keep looking.

Dont settle. As with all matters of the heart, you'll know when you find it.

And like any great relationship, it just gets BETTER and BETTER as the years roll on.

STEVE JOBS

I had no idea when I went to COLLEGE what I'd be doing...

I took many courses and participated in as many ACTIVITIES as I could. I learned A LOT about EVERY SINGLE THING.

MARTHA STEWART

It is never too late to be what you might have been.

GEORGE ELIOT

PROCRAS

30

TiNATiON

It's so tempting to wait until tomorrow to do what you should do today. While that idea might be ok once in a while, the habit of pushing things off until tomorrow will ultimately backfire because soon enough, everything will be due tomorrow. A better strategy is to plan out your week and work on bigger projects in smaller pieces.

INSTEAD OF PROCRASTINATING I DARE YOU TO TAKE 5 MINUTES TO START

WHAT'S WORRYING YOU. IT WILL MAKE YOU FEEL MUCH BETTER. ERNESTO MEJIA

Do the best you can with what you have SOME of the TIME - it is better than waiting until you are perfect and doing nothing in the meantime.

JESS PETTITT

DOING things at the LAST MINUTE reminds us of the IMPORTANCE of doing things at the FIRST Minute.

MATSHONA
DHLIWAYO

YOU DON'T HAVE TO SEE THE WHOLE STAIRCASE, JUST TAKE the FIRST STEP.

MARTIN LUTHER KING, JR.

PROCRASTINATION

IS LIKE A CREDIT CARD;
it's
A LOT of **FUN**
UNTIL YOU GET
the BILL.

CHRISTOPHER PARKER

If you
don't do anything,
you simply end up
OVERWHELMED
by something
happening.
MATSURI HINO

A year
from NOW
you May wish
you had started
today.

KAREN
LAMB

SOMEDAY
IS NOT
A DAY
OF THE WEEK.

JANET DAILEY

31

You failed a test. You didn't get the internship you wanted. So what? It might feel like the end of the world right now, but it's only a minor setback in the long road of life. Don't let one setback stop you from moving forward. Let yourself grieve for some time, then get back on your feet and get going. Sometimes, failures can teach us some of life's best lessons.

SETBACKS/
FAILURES

THE BRICK
WALLS ARE THERE
FOR A REASON.
THE BRICK WALLS
ARE NOT THERE TO
KEEP US OUT. THE
BRICK WALLS ARE
US HOW BADLY WE

In the middle of Difficulty lies OPPORTUNITY.
ALBERT EINSTEIN

THERE TO SHOW

WANT SOMETHING.

RANDY PAUSCH

FAILURE is SO IMPORTANT.

WE speak about SUCCESS all the time. It is the ABILITY to RESIST FAILURE or USE FAILURE that often leads to greater Success.

I've met people who don't want to try for fear of FAILING.

J.K. ROWLING

It is FAILURE that gives you the proper PERSPECTIVE on SUCCESS.

ELLEN DEGENERES

IF YOU ARE GOING through HELL, KEEP GOING.

WINSTON CHURCHILL

I'VE FAILED OVER AND OVER AND OVER AND OVER AGAIN IN MY LIFE. AND THAT IS WHY I SUCCEED.

MICHAEL JORDAN

All of
my wounds
are also my
GIFTS. Instead
of being a victim
to my circumstances,
I choose to use my
experiences to

HELP and
INSPIRE
others.

VICKI ABADESCO

sleep

32

Ping

Your brain and body need sleep. Period. Don't rob yourself of this by staying out too late, binge-watching a show, or staring mindlessly at social media. Commit to getting 7-8 hours of sleep per night. Just like you would an appointment with a doctor, don't be late for your sleep appointment. Get a good night's sleep and start the next day fresh as a cucumber.

If you can't sleep,
then get up
and do
something
instead of
lying there and
worrying. It's the
WORRY that gets
you, not the
LOSS of
SLEEP.
DALE CARNEGIE

I DO MY BEST
THINKING AT NIGHT
WHEN EVERYONE ELSE IS
SLEEPING.
NO INTERUPTIONS.
NO NOISE.

I LIKE THE
FEELING OF
BEING AWAKE
WHEN
NO ONE
ELSE IS.

JENNIFER NIVEN

I love sleep.
MY LIFE
HAS A
TENDENCY
TO FALL APART WHEN I'M
AWAKE, YOU KNOW?
ERNEST HEMINGWAY

THE NICEST thing
for me is sleep,
then at Least I
CAN
dream.
MARILYN MONROE

Laugh and the world laughs with you,

Snore and you sleep alone.

ANTHONY
BURGESS

Each night when I go to Sleep, I die.

THE
BEST CURE FOR INSOMNIA is TO GET A LOT OF SLEEP.

W.C. FIELDS

and the next Morning, when I wake up, I am Reborn.

MAHATMA GANDHI

THERE is A TIME FOR MANY WORDS, AND THERE is ALSO A TIME FOR SLEEP.

HOMER

SOCIAL

33

media

We now live in a world with two conversations happening at the same time. One is online and the other in-person. The two worlds influence each other, so don't think that what you post online stays online because it could impact your school, career, and life. Just as with any tool, learn how to use social media to your advantage, and you'll get ahead of everyone else.

To succeed in a VIRUAL WORLD, you must be a DIGITAL maven, an INDIVIDUAL THAT HAS THE ABILITY TO CONNECT, COMMUNICATE, BUILD POSITIVE RELATIONSHIPS,

THEY LOVED YOUR G.P.A.

AND **LEAD** THROUGH **VARiOUS** DIGITAL AND SOCIAL PLATFORMS.
JOSHUA FREDENBURG

THEN THEY SAW YOUR TWEETS.
JOHN PATRICK THOMAS

228

JUST AS SOME INDIVIDUALS OVERLY USE SOCIAL MEDIA OR SHARE TOO MUCH TOO OFTEN, NOT USING SOCIAL MEDIA CAN ALSO BE A RED FLAG.

SOCIAL MEDIA IS NOT THE PLACE TO AIR YOUR DIRTY LAUNDRY.

ROCKELL BARTOLI

HIRING COMMITIES WANT TO SEE PROSPECTIVE HIRES ENGAGING WITH OTHERS, SHARING THOUGHTFUL INFORMATION AND DEMONSTRATING A PASSION FOR THEIR LIFE.

E. MICHELE RAMSEY

DON'T SAY ANYTHING ONLINE THAT YOU WOULDN'T WANT PLASTERED ON A BILLBOARD WITH YOUR FACE ON IT.

ERIN BURY

TAKING A BREAK FROM SOCIAL MEDIA ALLOWS INDIVIDUALS TO RESET THEIR RELATIONSHIP WITH TECHNOLOGY.

PAUL GORDON BROWN

STUDENTS CAN REALLY DEFINE THEMSELVES through THEIR ONLINE PRESENCE WITH A LITTLE BIT OF EFFORT, WHILE STILL POSTING ABOUT THE FUN, SILLY, AND SOMETIMES WILD COLLEGIATE ACTIVITIES.

MELANIE
LEDBETTER-REMY

Social Media is a game that the UNINTENTIONAL will always loose, and the INTENTIONAL will always WIN.

The DIFFERENCE IS THE UNINTENTIONAL ARE USED BY SOCIAL MEDIA, AND THE INTENTIONAL PUT SOCIAL MEDIA TO USE. GEO DERICE

SPIRIT

RELI

34

UALITY
GION

A big part of the college experience is also personal growth. Who are you? Who do you want to be? What is your purpose for living? These are all big questions that will float around in your head while cramming to study for a midterm. You probably won't find every answer you want, but be ready for the questions to show up, because they will.

Everything you NEED in LIFE will be SECURED if you FIND YOUR PUROSE, LIVE OUT YOUR PURPOSE and FOCUS on MANIFESTING YOUR FOCUS EVERYDAY.

JOSHUA FREDENBURG

COLLEGE PROVIDES THiS GREAT PLATFORM To CULTiVATE the SPiRiT AND explore THESE iSSUES WiTH OTHER people.

SERENA WONG

At some point every one of us has asked the BIG QUESTiONS SURROUNDING our existence:

WHAT is THE MEANING OF LIFE?

AM I HEADED TOWARDS A SPECIFIC DESTiNATION?

IS MY LIFE iNHERENTLY PuRPoSEFUL AND VALUABLE?

Through the medium of SPiRiTUALiTY, people eNTERTAIN these questions and even attempt to resolve them. DILYS CHIEW

We're the ones who *decide,

WHEN I WAS IN COLLEGE, I MAJORED IN COMPARATIVE RELIGION BECAUSE I REALLY WANTED TO FIGURE OUT IF THERE WAS GOD AND HOW I SHOULD LIVE MY LIFE.

MARSHALL CURRY

MAINTAINING
SPIRITUALITY AND HUMANISM
ARE THE KEYS TO SUCCESS.
IT'S A BALANCE.
BIKRAM CHOUDHURY

'DO I hate
or am I
filled with love
...
do I think only about
myself or do I care for
others?'
... There are no limits
to our ambitions as
human beings.
JIMMY CARTER

I Think we have to be CAREFUL ABOUT WHAT WE LABEL AS A PREREQUISITE FOR SPIRITUALITY.

I don't think you have to KNOW A LOT to have a SPIRITUAL LIFE, BUT KNOWING GIVES LIFE RICHNESS.

OLYMPIA DUKAKIS

239

IT'S IMPORTANT TO BE
RELIGIOUS AND SPIRITUAL
in COLLEGE BECAUSE
STUDENTS NEED TO RELY
ON SOMETHING THAT is
UNCONDITIONAL AND
THAT WILL ALWAYS BE
THERE.

WE CAN'T RELY ON OUR
PARENTS TO ALWAYS
HELP US OUT, SO
RELYING ON FAITH CAN
SOLVE ANY PROBLEM.
HOLLY JENKINS

The End

About Tom Krieglstein

On December 5th 1980, Tom was born on a farm in Michigan where he spent the first nine years of his life. In 1999, Tom graduated high school with a stellar "C" grade point average, which led him to getting rejected from almost every bigger named college he applied to. In the end, Tom enrolled at a local community college named College of DuPage. While in college, Tom discovered himself and his passion for life by getting involved in his school's co-curricular activities. It was from Tom's co-curricular activities that he grew his initial interest in Student Affairs, Student Leadership, and community engagement.

During Tom's time at College of DuPage, he was honored as a Phi Theta Kappa All-USA Academic First Team Member, Illinois Centennial Scholar, and Outstanding Graduate.

In 2001, Tom entered his final two years of college at Aurora University where he graduated top of his class in Business Management and gave the commencement speech at graduation.

After a few false starts at becoming a full time professional speaker, Tom partnered with Kevin Prentiss, during their time working at Quantum Learning Network, to launch Swift Kick in 2004 and their award winning student leadership program, Dance Floor Theory. Through Tom's work in higher education, he also created The Student Affairs Collective and the NYEdTech Meetup.

On the personal side, Tom lives in New York City with his wife and step-daughter. He was also named after a cat, loves peanut butter so much he almost started a peanut butter festival, and is known to enjoy vermiculture.

In College

Now

Tom@SwiftKickHQ.com

@TomKrieglstein

Made in the USA
Las Vegas, NV
14 December 2021